Learn Thai Alphabet

with

Memory Aids to Your Great Adventure

by Russ Crowley & Duangta Wanthong Mondi

Published by Russ Crowley

Memory Aids To Your Great Adventure

www.learnthaialphabet.com

ISBN 978-1-908203-14-4 (paperback own ISBN)
ISBN 978-1496095817 (CreateSpace own ISBN)
ISBN 978-1-908203-16-8 (ebk)

All translations by Duangta Wanthong Mondi
All illustrations by Toni Howard

Read What Others Have Said About Our Products

I have achieved more than I would have thought possible in such a short space of time. Your colour code and picture aids make learning so much easier and it's so easy to refresh my memory from your app. I must say Russ, for me your product has been a great help, well worth the small price paid, and, would wholeheartedly recommend it to anyone wanting to learn to read and write Thai.

Orville Earle, London, UK, 17th October 2013

The Thai language is very intimidating and this program has taken the fear away! I would give it an 11 out of 10 points!! Thanks Russ!

Sandra Ching, Ecuador, 9th September 2013

I agree that your app and those posts are like a speed-of-light catalyst in terms teaching one the Thai script and reading it within literally two days (in my experience) which I find extraordinary!... I am just extremely excited that I have finally found material that does not throw one into the deep end of things.

Emiliusz Smorczewski, Illinois, USA, 9th July 2013

I have been very pleased with how quickly I have been able to learn and retain so much. Another aspect to purchasing is the quality of service received. The iPad version is awesome because I can use it anywhere without internet. I travel a lot and often am without internet, so it makes it nice.

Brian Atwell, USA, 3rd October 2013

Your book made learning the pronunciation and alphabet very easy. Thanks again.

Allen Mitchell, 9th April 2013

Your teaching technique is very good, much better than the other books I've seen.

Julian Wheeler, Chonburi, Thailand, 28th October 2012

This is the best help I've had, thank you so much, really easy to understand.

Rebekah Wilkes, UK, 7th May 2013

I'm surprised at how quickly and easily this is all sinking in. Thanks for making it easy.

Mitch Costello, Sydney, Australia, 9th September 2013

These resources are making the learning of Thai a reality after numerous false starts... the simplicity of the system breaks down the psychological barriers to attacking the idea of reading/writing Thai.

Brock Estes, Richmond, VA, 15th September 2012

Table of Contents

Numbers

Appendix

Quest

Welcome to QuEST

Welcome to **QuEST: Quick, Easy, Simple Thai** and to volume 2, **Learn Thai Alphabet with Memory Aids to Your Great Adventure**.

We believe that starting to learn a new language is akin to starting an adventure. With learning Thai, not only will this be an exciting journey into a foreign land, but it's an exploration into a country that is more than likely vastly different from that of your own; and, the mixture of trepidation and excitment you are perhaps feeling helps to make this both thrilling and unique.

Indeed, many peole baulk at the thought of trying to learn Thai script, preferring rather to concentrate on speaking and using transliterated Thai. All of this is fine of course – Thai's *LOVE* to hear foreigners speak, or try to speak, their language; but, by buying this book, you are not only committing yourself to wanting to learn more about Thailand's language, but you are showing you are interested in wanting to learn more about her country, her culture, and her people; and, this is a whole new adventure.

Indeed, setting off down this side-road will not only allow you to delve deeper into the essence of Thailand, but you will find that, as you continue to travel and the more you explore, you will be amazed at what lies around the next corne and is revealed as more paths open up before you – these series of small adventures then help to make up an entire *Quest - Quick, Easy, Simple Thai.*

What is Quest?

Quest is our methodology for teaching you Thai. Consisting of 4 volumes, Quest takes you from a beginner, with zero knowledge of the Thai language, through to being able to read Thai.

Volume I - Learning Thai, Your Great Adventure is the place to start your Quest. Introducing the Thai language, the alphabet: the consonants, classes and sounds, vowels, tone, why it's important; and so much more.

Volume II - Learn Thai Alphabet with Memory Aids to Your Great Adventure is the book that makes learning the Thai alphabet so simple: it couldn't get any easier.

Volume III - The Perfect Thai Phrasebook is for those who not only want an accompaniment on their trip to the Land of Smiles, but is for those who, when they realise (as you did) that they want to learn more about Thailand, its language and its culture, can then use it as an aide-memoir to learning to read Thai: packed with everyday words, phrases, and expressions, that people actually use.

Volume IV - How to Read Thai is the book that makes reading Thai not only a reality, but easy. We guide you step-by-step through the process of breaking down Thai sentences into words, and words into syllables. It might sound crazy, but Thai has few spaces and puntuation and the answer to the common question of, *"Where or how do you even start?"* is a mystery no longer.

Of course, learning the Thai alphabet is quite difficult for some and, as there is *no one size fits all* teaching method, we also have *The Learn Thai alphabet application*, which is based on this book and is web-based (so works on your PC, Mac and iPad). You can see more about this on page 19.

The Thai Alphabet

You've decided to make the step to learn the Thai alphabet, you've settled down with your brand new study book, you've read the introductory chapter and know how best to use the book; and, you then begin learning Thai. This is fantastic news!

Quite soon afterwards, you realise that the only way you're going to be able to learn and retain the alphabet is by using 'flash cards'. Then, you can either make your own, or you can purchase some of the excellent cards available in Thailand, great stuff!

Once done, you then work through the Middle Class group of consonants and learn all 9 of them, then you move on to the High Class consonants (11 of), and then onto the final set, Low Class (24 of).

You've cracked it and can recognise all of the 44 consonants in the Thai alphabet. You start reading some 'easier' words in Thai and then, as is bound to happen, you come across a word you don't understand; and, the girl speaking on the mp3 pronounces the sound as a /t/ and you're sure it's an /s/.

Confused?

Unfortunately, it's a fairly common occurrence, but the situation arises because some Thai consonants have a different sound depending on whether they are an *initial* or a *final consonant* in a syllable or word.

The problem is, you have to learn all of these and it's not necessarily easy to do. To be honest with you, it can drive you barmy; it can take a while, and banging your head against the wall will probably achieve little more that give you a sore head.

There is a much easier way though; and, that is using *Quest* and this book. We will help you to learn the sounds the consonants and vowels of the Thai Alphabet make, plus all the other elements you <u>need</u> to know - *Quick, Easy, Simple Thai - Quest.*

Our Method

Russ read *'How to Learn Any Language"* by *Barry Farber* a few years ago, and one of the excellent techniques that he covers is *Harry Lorayne's, Magic Memory Aid*. This is a trick where you use acronyms, mnemonics, and associations with an event (fictitious or otherwise) that helps you recall that information.

It's a brilliant method because creating the association yourself makes it even more memorable to you, and thereby easier to remember and recall.

There's one particular example that Russ uses to explain memory association and that's how he always used to get the Thai words for *school* and *hotel* mixed up: one is called *rong raem* and the other is *rong rian*; but, which is which? (Note: in our transliteration system we write raem as rɛɛm).

Well, *school is rong rian* and *hotel* is *rong rɛɛm* (this sounds quite close to *rong rem*, but stretch the 'rɛɛm' part out).

He always had difficulty remembering which was which, until he came up with a 'scenario' to help: he remembers being on rugby tour a few years ago and after the conclusion of the days antics, visualised getting back to the hotel late at night in the dark and, stumbling about, accidently entering the *'wrong room'* - *rong rem*: *hotel / rong rɛɛm / wrong room* - **simple!**

Okay, you may be thinking this is a bit lame, but the beauty of this kind of association is the link only needs to be tenuous and the chances are you will never ever forget it.

Ramkamhaeng University, Bangkok

How Do We Do It?

Fortunately for you though, we're not going to give you lots of anecdotes or stories to help you remember. We're actually going to make this even simpler by giving you pictures instead; our brains work in pictures so, in the first instance, remembering a picture makes the entire process far easier.

Now our assumption is that you're reading this book because you're struggling to learn the Thai alphabet sounds. Notice we don't say *'learn the Thai alphabet'* – if you've learnt the names of all the consonants then it would be a bit strange you getting this book – we learn the sounds.

We'll start with the consonants as you have to learn these before you go onto the vowels. You may or may not have realised that the Thai alphabet is different to the English alphabet in a number of ways. The first, and most obvious is the script; but, don't cringe, we agree it may look daunting but trust us you can and will do it.

How do we know you can do it? Simply because Russ did it. He failed miserably at French, Spanish, and German even though he already knew their alphabets; and, if he can learn Thai, then so can **anyone**.

The second big difference with the Thai alphabet is consonants and vowels don't mix. In the Roman alphabet, there are A, B, C, D, E, F... and the vowels are right in there, 5 out of 26.

However, what is confusing for a lot of non-native Brits is the sounds these vowels make: we have 5 vowels but they make something like 19 different sounds (plus we've got the consonants which sound like vowels, such as the *'i'* in *heavy* [*hev'i*]); so, as you can see, the problems aren't all one way.

The good news is, in Thai, consonants and vowels stay separate; and, this is actually very handy when you consider there are 44 consonants and 32 vowels (the bad news). But, there's nothing wrong with a challenge and the fact that some of the consonants make different sounds when in a different syllable position doesn't bother us in the slightest.

Also, when you also consider that Thai is a tonal language and you therefore have to learn and remember whether each consonant is either Low class, Middle class or High class, that doesn't put us off either; and, do you know why it doesn't? It's because we have a plan and, in the words of Edmund Blackadder, it's even better as it's not just any old plan, it's a cunning plan!

Central to our cunning plan are the simple pictures we use: each simple picture has everything in it to tell you what you need to know about the particular letter of the alphabet.

So, going back to Russ's problem with *rong rɛɛm* and *rong riian*, rather than us telling you he's walking down a dark corridor, fumbling for his key, groping for the door handle...the key doesn't work, he tries again, makes lots of noise in the process, the door opens, then he realises...blah, blah, blah, we think you get the idea.

All of this takes too long to tell you; but, if we have a simple picture which shows all of this information, then recalling this picture is far faster than going through the process just mentioned; and, this is how we teach you the Thai alphabet – simple pictures with just the information you need.

For example, the first letter of the Thai alphabet is ก . As a beginner, you're not that interested in what it's actually called (though this is important to know, you can always work on it later), you just want to know what sounds it makes so you can begin speaking and reading Thai.

If you were paying attention you'll have noticed I said sound**s**, not sound. This particular consonant makes two different sounds: it makes one sound when it's the initial consonant of a syllable and it makes another totally different sound when it's a final (or terminal) consonant of a syllable.

Even more horrified? I hope not! Remember, we still have our cunning plan...

We personally think that you can learn the consonants in a few hours on one day and then learn the vowels the next day. If you then spread it about over a few days, we are 100% sure you can easily grasp everything in this book quickly. If you have a photographic memory, you're laughing but, if like us, you just have a normal memory, it will take a little longer.

As Brock said:

> *"How simple an idea in Memory Aids!!"*

Method

Right then, how do we do it?

Here we have a picture of a knight. Now, this knight is not just any old knight, he's actually one of the most virtuous and famous knights of them all: it's Galahad, one of King Arthur's knights from the Arthurian Legend of King Arthur and his Round Table.

But, '*Galahad, a knight of King Arthur and his Round Table*' is a bit of a mouthful to remember so we'll shorten it to something easier: Galahad Knight.

This is the name for this gallant warrior: Galahad Knight.

Now, *Galahad Knight* provides us with all the information we need to be able to recognise the Thai consonant - ก .

It also gives us the initial consonant sound and the final consonant sound. How?

To show you, we superimpose the Thai consonant shape ก onto the image. This then gives us:

That's not 100% clear, so we'll zoom in a little bit:

Now you can see how the shape of the consonant conforms to the front-edge of Galahad Knights' shield, his torso, and his helmet: even where the visor on the helmet matches the '*beak*' of the consonant.

So, how does this help us?

- Well, from the picture name, we take the initial letter of the first word to be the sound the consonant makes when it's an **initial consonant**: Galahad

- The initial letter of the second word is the sound the consonant makes when it's a **final consonant**: Knight.

ก makes the **G** sound (or /**g**/ sound) when it's acting as an initial consonant, and it makes the **K** sound (/**k**/ sound) when it's a final consonant.

If you already own *Learning Thai, Your Great Adventure*, then you'll know that not all consonants have a different initial and final [consonant] sound. Some only have one sound. Where this is the case, our picture title only has one word. **One word = one sound**. It couldn't get any easier could it?

This means that if you see a single sound consonant, it **always** makes the same sound irrespective of where it is in a syllable. You'll see the image, you'll remember the title, et voila... you have the consonant sound.

To illustrate this, in our next example, we have a picture of a kangaroo:

We also have this consonant: ญ . Can you guess the sound this consonant makes?

Again (and as always), we superimpose the consonant onto the picture, and we see that the actual consonant shape conforms to the shape of our **K**angaroo:

As there is only one word for this picture, this consonant **always** makes the /**k**/ sound, regardless of whether it is in the initial or in the final consonant position is a syllable or word.

Class of Consonant

The only other thing you have to remember about a consonant is its class. **Every** consonant belongs to one of three classes: High, Middle or Low. The problem is, how can we remember which consonant is in which class? Again, we have our plan.

If you have *LTYGA* you'll have already seen this, but every consonant picture will have either a red, yellow or green background which corresponds to its consonant class. We know, you may be thinking there's too much to take in, but we've once again made it very simple to remember:

So there you have it:

* **Red** is High Class.

* Yellow is Middle Class (I know this is orange, but yellow doesn't stand out on a white page; where you see orange, please assume yellow).

* **Green** is Low Class.

Now, with our hero in the first example, we know he's a Middle Class consonant so he'll need a yellow background.

Imagine Galahad Knight in the desert and following what we already know:

* Initial Consonant sound = /**g**/ (**G**alahad)

* Final consonant sound = /**k**/ (**K**night.)

* Consonant class/background: Yellow = Middle Class consonant.

With our antipodean friend, we see him bounding across the Australian outback with the sun setting over a scorching desert.

Here we have:

- **K**angaroo (one word, one sound)= /**k**/ (**K**angaroo)

- Red background = High Class consonant.

Great stuff, only 42 more consonants to go.

How to Use This Book

The consonants have been grouped by consonant class to help you learn and remember them. The Middle Class is the smallest group, with 9 consonants; then the High Class group, with 11; and, then finally the Low Class group, with 24. The consonant groups will be in this order.

We recommend downloading the *Flash Cards* and printing out the Middle Class consonants. You can download the flash cards at:

http://www.learnthaialphabet.com/flashcards

When you have these, cut them along the border lines, put them in one pile (in the order that they're in) and to one side.

Then, go to page 23 and start with the Middle Class consonants. Go through these slowly, one at a time, repeating the picture title (out loud if possible). Do this three or four times then move onto the next picture.

Go through all 9 Middle Class consonants two or three times then put the book to one side. Pick up your flash cards and turn the top one over. Now you see the consonant shape you should be able to recall the picture **and** its name. Repeat the name of it, et voila, you've just recalled the name. Remember the picture background? What colour was it? Now you know its class.

Repeat this until you've finished the Middle Class then move onto the High Class and so forth. Once you've been through them all, jumble your flash cards up and practise, practise, practise.

We're confident that you can learn the consonants in as little as a couple of hours but, as always, it depends on the individual and their learning ability.

Also, though we teach you to learn the Thai alphabet in this manner, once you're proficient, it is a good idea to start learning the actual proper Thai names. As such, the full list of consonants is in Appendix A. at the back of this book.

Before we move onto the alphabet, we'll just have a look at our Learn Thai Alphabet Application.

The Learn Thai Alphabet Application

The Learn Thai Alphabet application is web-based app and works on either the PC or a MAC (plus it works on the iPad 2+). It is based on this book but has interactive quizzes, hints and tips, all the alphabet sounds by native Thai speakers, and much more. If you prefer a more  interactive learning experience, then this is for you. Click here to check it out: click to instantly try out Trial Version.

It's available from our website at **www.learnthaialphabet.com**.

Also, if you buy the web application, you also get a **free** copy of the **Learn Thai Alphabet with Memory Aids to Your Great Adventure** pdf ebook.[1]

Okay, lets learn the alphabet, Middle class consonants first...

---

1. If you've already bought the paperback or actually have the ebook and then decide you'd also like to get the app, then email us on support@learnthaialphabet.com and we'll sort you out a large discount.

Consonants

Middle Class Consonants

ก Galahad Knight

= Galahad **K**night

Here we have **G**alahad **K**night (/**g**/ when the consonant is an initial consonant and /**k**/ when it is a final consonant[a]) on a yellow background (denoting it as a Middle Class consonant).

a. You may be thinking that the /k/ sound here is more of an 'n' sound, but Russ is a big Monty Python fan and is using their 'kerrr-niggit' version.

จ Jabberwocky Tail

= Jabberwocky **T**ail

Next, we have a **J**abberwocky [with a long] **T**ail: /**j**/ as an initial consonant and /**t**/ as a final consonant. The yellow background again denotes a Middle Class consonant.

From hereon, we won't refer to '*as an initial or final consonant*' or to the colour of the background and what it denotes in the explanation text. If you need reminding, re-read the introduction.

ฎ Dog Treat

= **D**og **T**reat

A **D**og sitting on the steps, begging for a **T**reat

ฏ Dog Treat

= **D**og **T**reat

Again, the same **D**og begging for another **T**reat

ด Damsel Tower

= **D**amsel **T**ower

A young **D**amsel, alone in a **T**ower

ต Damsel Tower

= **D**amsel **T**ower

The same **D**amsel alone in a [slightly different shaped] Tower

บ Bald Patch

= **B**ald **P**atch

A man with a **B**ald **P**atch thinking about going for a paddle

ป - Bottom Pit

= **B**ottom **P**it

A man sitting at the **B**ottom of a **P**it

อ Awful

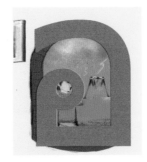

= **Aw**ful

Staring out of the window at the **Aw**ful weather

High Class Consonants

ข Kangaroo

= **K**angaroo

A **K**angaroo against a red setting sky (**Red** background = **High Class**)

ฃ Karaoke

= **K**araoke

A lady singing **K**araoke down by the marina

ฉ Cat's Tail

= Chat's **T**ail

If you know any French, their word for cat is chat. And with it's long tail we have **Ch**at's **T**ail

ฐ Tassles

= Tassles

The **T**assles on a Greek Hoplites' helmet

ถ Tails

= Tails

A gentleman in **T**ails at the ball

ผ Profit

= **P**rofit

The **P**rofit sheet of a business

ฝ Fruit Picking

= **F**ruit **P**icking

Fruit **P**icking berries

ศ Sign Top

= **S**ign **T**op

Follow the **S**ign to the **T**op

ษ Sea Trip

= **S**ea **T**rip

Sea **T**rip

ส Squirrel Tail

= **S**quirrel **T**ail

A **S**quirrel with a long **T**ail eating a nut

ห Humps

= **H**umps

Humps

Low Class Consonants

ค Koala

= **K**oala

A **K**oala holding onto a tree branch (**Green** background = **Low Class**)

ฅ Koala

= **K**oala

Another **K**oala

ฆ Kite

= **K**ite

Kite

ৰ Guarding

= guardi**NG**

guardi**NG** - this consonant makes the **/ng/** sound

ৰ Chef Tasting

= **Ch**ef **T**asting

Chef **T**asting

ৰ Sax Twins

= **S**ax **T**wins

The **S**axophone **T**wins

ฌ Child Tantrum

= **Ch**ild **T**antrum

A **Ch**ild having a **T**antrum

ญ You're Nicked

= **Y**ou're **N**icked

"**Y**ou're **N**icked!"

ฏ Tortoise

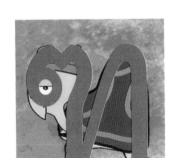

= **T**ortoise

A cute little **T**ortoise

ฒ Training

= **T**raining

Training

ณ Napoleon

= **N**apoleon

Napoleon

ท Typist

= **T**ypist

Typist

ธ Teabag

  = **T**eabag

Teabag

น Navigating

  = **N**avigating

[Planning a sailing trip] **N**avigating

พ Praying

  = **P**raying

Praying

ฟ Finished Picking

  = **F**inished **P**icking

Back for more berries but I think he's **F**inished **P**icking.

ภ Painting

  = **P**ainting

Painting

ม Map

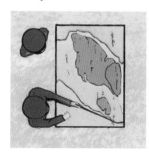  = **M**ap

Two General's planning on a **M**ap

ย Yeti Ice

= **Y**eti **I**ce

A **Y**eti on **I**ce [skates]

ร Rabbit Nibbling

= **R**abbit **N**ibbling

A **R**abbit **Ni**bbling at a small carrot

ล Large Nugget

= **L**arge **N**ugget

"Yeeee, haaaa!" Struck Gold! He's found a **L**arge **N**ugget.

ว Wave over

= Wave **O**ver

"Where did that come from!" A large **W**ave **O**ver the bow of the boat.

ฬ Look Nice

= Look **N**ice

A pretty young lady making herself **L**ook **N**ice

ฮ Hooray

= Hooray

I think he's just won? "**H**ooray!"

Your Notes

Vowels

Simple Vowels

Unlike consonant sounds, vowels don't belong to any class so you only have to remember the sounds they make.

Please bear in mind that the sounds these vowels make (from the pictures) are as close as the English language allows us to get to the actual Thai sound. We have checked and verified all these using the Cambridge phonetic system.

Thai uses two types of vowel: short vowels and long vowels. With the trans-literation system that we use in the book *Learning Thai, Your Great Adventure* we differentiate between short and long vowels by doubling up on the vowel when it is long. For example, when you see the drawing *bed*, even though the sound is the /e/ part of *bed*, the actual Thai sound we are trying to produce/replicate is a long vowel and, as it's a long vowel, we double-up when we write it: /ee/. Please note though, it is still pronounced /e/ it's just a longer, drawn-out sound. We hope that hasn't confused you too much. So, without further ado:

-ำ = This vowel makes the /am/ sound as in umbrella

ใ- = This vowel makes the /ai/ sound as in knight.

  ไ - = /ai/ as in **fly**.

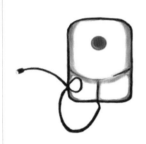  เ-า = /ou/ as in **mouse**

  - ะ = /a/ as in **puffin**

- ∩ = /**aa**/ as in p**a**lm

= /**i**/ as in l**i**p

= /**ii**/ as in st**ee**ple

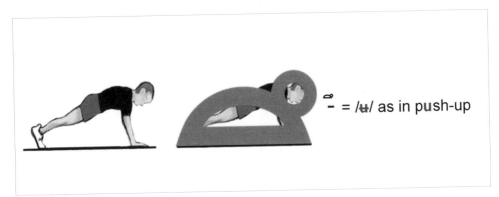

ึ = /ɨ/ as in push-up

ื = /ɨɨ/ as in bloom

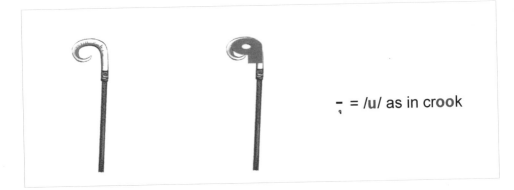

ุ = /u/ as in crook

  = /uu/ as in boot

  = /e/ as in net

  = /ee/ as in bed

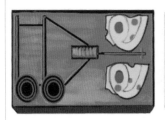 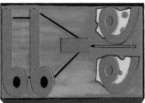

แ - ะ = /ɛ/ as in trap

แ - = /ɛɛ/ as in mare

โ - ะ = /o/ as in cot

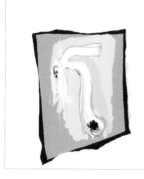  โ - = /oo/ as in gh**o**st

  เ - าะ = /ɔ/ as in sl**o**t

 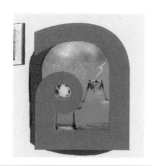 - อ = /ɔɔ/ as in **aw**ful

You may have noticed that อ is also a consonant, it is. Whichever function or role it is providing, it still makes the same sound. For further explanation you'll need *Learning Thai, Your Great Adventure* or *How to Read Thai*.

That concludes the simple vowels, now we'll have a look at the complex vowels.

Complex Vowels

When we refer to complex vowels we mean vowels which are composed of more than one sound, i.e. dipthongs or tripthongs (two or three sounds respectively). We have quite a few dipthongs in the English language but not too many tripthongs, Thai has a few more. Thank you in advance for bearing with our diagrams and descriptions below, it took us quite a while to come up with the right pictures that would accurately represent the sounds and the vowel shapes; we hope they help you.

เ - อ = /əə/ as in **early**

เ-ีย = /iia/ as in **rein-deer**

เ-ือ = /ʉʉa/ as in **skua**

◌ัว = /ua/ as in p**ure**

ฤ ◌ = /r~~ɯ~~/ as in **roo**k

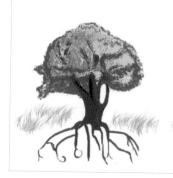

ฤๅ ◌ = /r~~ɯɯ~~/ as in **roo**t

ฎ - = /lɯ/ as in **loo**kout

ฎๅ - = /lɯɯ/ as in **loo**ney

There are 4 complex vowels that are extremely rare and you will hardly ever see them in modern language. These are covered in Appendix D. on page 72.

Where to Write Vowels

As you probably know, and are perhaps confused by, Thai vowels are written before, above, after and below consonants. Shock, gasp, horror, confused? Don't be, it's very straightforward.

With few exceptions (four to be precise: ใ -, ◌ั -, ฤ -, ฤๅ -), when a vowel contains a loop, the loop <u>always</u> points in the direction of where the consonant is written. So, when you see เ it points to the right. This means the consonant is written to the right of it (the vowel): เ -.

Vowels Before

These vowels all have loops that point **at** the consonant; therefore, these are written to the left (in front) of the consonant they 'belong' to:

เ -, แ -, ใ -, โ -, ฤ -, ฤๅ -

Vowels Below

These two vowels have loops that point up, so they are written underneath the consonant they 'belong to':

◌ุ , ◌ู (We've drawn these much larger than those shown previously you can see them clearly).

Vowels Above

Vowels that are written above the consonants need to have a base, and preferably a flat base; four out of the five do.We like to think that the fifth one 'is getting there: one day it will be flat, but it isn't hasn't made it just yet:

◌ิ ◌ี ◌ื ◌ึ ◌ั This last vowel (◌ั) is not shown in this book as it's the same as the vowel, - ะ , just written in a different position. We don't cover it here but it's explained in *Learning Thai, Your Great Adventure* and *How to Read Thai*.

Vowels After

Those vowels that come after the consonant always point (with the curved bit) at the consonant. Remember that the loops point 'at' the consonant:

-ิๅ ,- ๅ , - ะ

That's it, that's all the vowels. Remember, the individual vowel components are **always** written in the same place.

Flashcards

Also remember, that you can download all the flash cards at:

http://www.learnthaialphabet.com/flashcards

Tone

Tone

Thai is a tonal language and every syllable will have one of five tones: high, low, middle, falling or rising.

Because the Thai language is tonal, changing the tone of a syllable or a word changes it's meaning. You now know that more than one consonant makes the /**ch**/ sound, the /**s**/ sound, the /**p**/ sound, etc. So how do we actually know which consonant to use?

Well this is one of the difficulties with learning Thai, especially learning to write Thai. The vowels are fairly straightforward but the fact that within a consonant **class** there are sometimes more than one consonant making a particular sound, this can prove difficult. Ultimately, you have to learn each individual word. It is a laborious process but not insurmountable by any means. Children do it, why can't we?

Before we look into this, we need to know that there are four factors that affect syllable tone, these are:

1. Does the syllable have a tone mark above the initial consonant?
2. What is the class of the consonant (remember, each consonant must belong to either **High**, Middle or **Low** class)?
3. Is the vowel length long or short?
4. Does the end [consonant] sound make this a *live syllable* or a *dead syllable* (refer to *Learning Thai, Your Great Adventure or How to Read Thai*?)

Point number 1 is the overriding factor here: If the syllable has a tone mark, you can forget about the other rules.

Tone Marks

There are four tone marks in Thai script and, in conjunction with the consonant class help, these determine what the syllable tone is. These are as follows:

Tone Mark	When written above the consonant class (shown below), that syllable will produce the tone shown:		
	Low Class	Middle Class	High Class
่	Falling Tone (^)	Low (\\)	Low (\\)
้	High Tone (/)	Falling (^)	Falling (^)
๊	High (/)		
๋	Rising Tone (v)		

How To Use the Table

If your syllable has one of the above tone marks above the initial consonant, you then need to identify the consonant class of the initial consonant (High, Middle or Low class). Once you have done this, you cross reference it in the table to get the syllable tone.

Some of you may think that this is difficult to remember (for Russ it was) so he came up with the following pictures and text to help him.

Remembering Tone Mark Rules

Mái èek (̄)

This looks like a bomb dropped from a warplane.

- When the plane flies on *high* or *middle* altitude bombing missions (*high* or *middle* class consonants) the bomb explodes at *low level* (read *low tone*).

- When the plane is on a *low* altitude bombing mission (read *low* class consonant) it uses pinpoint accuracy and can drop the bomb into holes and the bomb *falls* deeper into the ground (read *falling* tone).

Therefore:

Middle & **High** [class consonants] = **Low** [tone]; **Low** [class consonant] = **Falling** [tone].

Mái too (˘)

Imagine this as the head of a sickle (or a scythe) used in a peasant rebellion.

The **low class** peasants revolt and cut the heads off of the *middle* and *high* classes who all *fall* from grace and the *low* classes now elevate themselves to the new, vacant *high* class.

Therefore: **Middle** & **High** = **Fall**ing, **Low** = [the new] **High.**

Picture in your mind the shape of a sickle used in the 1917 Russian Revolution.

Mái dtrii (˘)

Imagine this shape as a crown on the head of royalty - the *high*est level (**high** tone with all consonant classes).

Mái jàt-dtà-waa (⁺‾)

This is like a *rising* star, twinkling in the night sky (**rising** tone with all consonant classes).

That's much easier to remember! But, how do we determine tone if there isn't a tone mark?

Determining Tone

If the syllable doesn't have a tone mark then you have to calculate the syllable tone. This is one of the things that puts people off learning the language, as it can be very difficult (and slow) to work out the tone of each syllable: it doesn't have to be though; but, before we show you the easy way, we'll go through the standard method.

First, we'll reiterate on what information we need.

Here are the factors that you need to know to calculate a syllable tone:

1. The class of the consonant
2. Whether the vowel is short or long, and
3. Whether the final consonant is a *sonorant* or *stop* final (Appendix C).

	Consonant Class		
Syllable Type	**High Class**	**Middle Class**	**Low Class**
Dead Syllables	Low Tone (\\)	Low Tone (\\)	Short Vowel: High Tone (/)
			Long Vowel: Falling Tone (^)
Live Syllables	Rising Tone (v)	Middle Tone	Middle Tone

As you can see from the table, *for Low Class consonants only*, if the syllable is dead, the tone will depend on whether the vowel is short or long.

Complicated? Of course it is. It's also very difficult to work out - this way. But, as always, we have a much easier method to help you and that is by remembering a few simple acronyms.

Remembering How to Calculate Tone

Here are the ones that Russ created and uses to remember the tone rules:

- Harry Drinks Lager (High [class consonant] + Dead [syllable] = Low [tone]) HDL

- Harry Likes Red Stripe (High + Live = Rising) HLR

- Mike Drinks Lager (Middle + Dead = Low) MDL

- Mike Likes Miller (Middle + Live = Middle) MLM

- Lesley Drinks SHandy (Low + Dead + Short [vowel] = High) LDSH

- Lesley Drinks Lager Fast (Low + Dead + Long [vowel] = Falling) LDLF

- Lesley Likes Miller (Low + Live = Middle) LLM

Remember these and you'll never have to refer to the table again.[1] Also, we use the same names, the same colour-coding, the same acronyms across our entire system; so, once you've learnt them, they never change and the rest is easy!

---

1. Now you've probably noticed that these acronyms have a slight alcoholic slant towards them. The reason for this is it helps me remember them (the acronyms, not the alcohol). It is actually a proven fact that the more raunchy or saucier the link is between the item you are trying to remember and the story, picture or aid you use to actually remember it is, the easier it is to recall.

Your Notes

Numbers

Numbers

Unless you go off the beaten track in Thailand, you are likely to see familiar Arabic numerals (0 - 9). If you're in an area where English is not particularly common then it will help you to know what the Thai numerals actually are.

๐	0	๕	5
๑	1	๖	6
๒	2	๗	7
๓	3	๘	8
๔	4	๙	9

The number 0, easy to remember and recall.

Imagine it's a big barrel chest and the guy's been told he's won. he points at his chest, and says,

"I've won?" (one)

2

A ball bounces twice before it hits the wall and rebounds down.

3

Somone attaches a loop to a 3 and, top-heavy, it falls over.

4

If you write the number 4 out very loosely, you could write it **exactly** like this.

If you add 1 [loop] to the number 4, you get 5.

Almost a mirror image of a 6.

Slightly harder, imagine a 7 has fallen over backwards, and then a fist comes up from below and grabs it.

A guilty cat walking away, looks back as if to say,

"It wasn't me who ate [eight] it, it was the dog."

A 9 has gone all floppy and fallen forward and it's shirt-tail flies in the wind.

Don't forget, with these numbers and the other memory aids, it's all about associating the shapes with the items you're trying to embed in your memory; and, though some of these might not particulalry resonate with you, if you can come up with your own, it's a far better and more effective way.

We've had feedback and some say that we should change this, or change that. We really appreciate, read, and listen to all the feedback we get, but again, this is what has worked for Russ and so many other people and isn't set in stone.

We hope that you can see how the thinnest of threads can make the link real and aid recollections. We encourage you to come up with your own, it makes your own learning far easier.

Appendix

Appendix A. Consonant List

Weve included the list of consonants that you've gone through here so that you can see the order they're actually in and the sounds they make. You can use this as a quick reference table. Refer to Appendix F. for the actual table with Thai names, what the actual name means, etc.

No.	Thai Character	Picture Name	Initial Consonant Sound	Final Consonant Sound
1	ก	Galahad Knight	/g/	/k/
2	ข	Kangaroo	/k/	
3	ฃ	Karaoke	/k/	
4	ค	Koala	/k/	
5	ฅ	Koala	/k/	
6	ฆ	Kite	/k/	
7	ง	guarding	/ng/	
8	จ	Jabberwocky Tail	/j/	/t/
9	ฉ	Chat Tail	/ch/	/t/
10	ช	Chef Tasting	/ch/	/t/
11	ซ	Saxophone Twins	/s/	/t/
12	ฌ	Child Tantrum	/ch/	/t/
13	ญ	You're Nicked	/y/	/n/
14	ฎ	Dog Treat	/d/	/t/
15	ฏ	Dog Treat	/dt/	/t/
16	ฐ	Tassles	/t/	
17	ฑ	Tortoise	/t/	
18	ฒ	Training	/t/	
19	ณ	Napoleon	/n/	

20	ด	Damsel Tower	/d/	/t/
21	ต	Damsel Tower	/dt/	/t/
22	ถ	Tails	/t/	
23	ท	Typist	/t/	
24	ธ	Teabag	/t/	
25	น	Navigating	/n/	
26	บ	Bald Patch	/b/	/p/
27	ป	Bottom Pit	/bp/	/p/
28	ผ	Profits	/p/	
29	ฝ	Fruit Picking	/f/	/p/
30	พ	Praying	/p/	
31	ฟ	Finished Picking	/f/	/p/
32	ภ	Painting	/p/	
33	ม	Map	/m/	
34	ย	Yeti Ice	/y/	/i/
35	ร	Rabbit Nibbling	/r/	/n/
36	ล	Large Nugget	/l/	/n/
37	ว	Wave Over	/w/	/o/
38	ศ	Sign Top	/s/	/t/
39	ษ	Sea Trip	/s/	/t/
40	ส	Squirrel Tail	/s/	/t/
41	ห	Humps	/h/	
42	ฬ	Look Nice	/l/	/n/
43	อ	Awful	/ɔɔ/	
44	ฮ	Hooray	/h/	

Appendix A.1 Patterns

You will be able to see some patterns in the initial and final consonant sounds in the above table:

- If the initial consonant sound is /**ch**/, /**d**/ or /**s**/ the final consonant sound is /**t**/
- If the initial consonant sound is /**b**/ or /**f**/, the final consonant sound is /**p**/
- If the initial consonant sound is /**l**/ or /**r**/, the final consonant sound is /**n**/.

Appendix B. Different Consonant Sounds

There are three consonants which, when they are in the *initial consonant* position, have no direct English equivalent, these are (in the drawings): ฎ (Dog Treat), ฏ (Damsel Tower) and ฏ (Bottom Pit).

The sounds are very similar to ฎ (Dog Treat), ฏ (Damsel Tower) and ฏ (Bald Patch) but are formed by two consonants pronounced together:

- ฎ (**Dog Treat**) = /dt/ (as in s**t**op)
- ฏ (**Damsel Tower**) = /dt/ (as in s**t**op)
- ฏ (**Bottom Pit**) = /bp/ (as in s**p**ot)

as opposed to:

- ฎ (**Dog Treat**) = /d/ (as in **d**og)
- ฏ (**Damsel Tower**) = /d/ (as in **d**og)
- ฏ (**Bald Patch**) = /b/ (as in **b**all)

At this stage, just recognising the consonants and associating the /**d**/ or /**b**/ sound is where you want to be; once you've got that, then work on the finer points above.

Appendix C. Stop or Sonorant Final Sounds

There are 8 final consonant sounds. Five of these are sonorant and three are stop final sounds. If you remember the stop final sounds, the remainder are all sonorant finals. The stop final consonant sounds are /k/, /p/ and /t/.

If all of this is too much to absorb at the moment, just use the following sentence to help you remember the stop final sounds:

Stop eating KP nuts as they stick in your Teeth.

Appendix D. Rare Vowels

For the purists among you, you will notice that we've only included 28 drawings for the vowels yet there are 32 vowels in the Thai language.

The main reason for this is that the excluded vowels are very uncommon; the second reason is we couldn't come up with an appropriate image for them. As such, the best thing to do is to learn the equivalent long vowel sounds and then shorten them is you encounter any of these. The remaining four are:

This vowel is very rare. Learn it's 'long' vowel equivalent and when you encounter the short vowel, recall the long vowel sound and make it short.

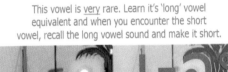

/ə/ as in above

เ - อะ = /ə/ as in above

This vowel is very rare. Learn it's 'long' vowel equivalent and when you encounter the short vowel, recall the long vowel sound and make it short.

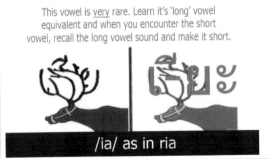

/ia/ as in ria

เ - ียะ = /ia/ as in ria

This vowel is <u>very</u> rare. Learn it's 'long' vowel equivalent and when you encounter the short vowel, recall the long vowel sound and make it short.

เ◌ี อะ = /ɯa/ as in **newer**

/ɯa/ as in newer

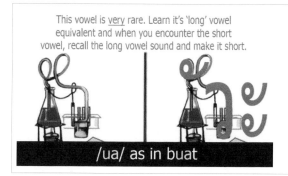

This vowel is <u>very</u> rare. Learn it's 'long' vowel equivalent and when you encounter the short vowel, recall the long vowel sound and make it short.

◌ัว ะ = /ua/ as in buat

/ua/ as in buat

Appendix E. Special Signs & Features

The Thai language has few punctuation marks or other 'signs'. The ones that you will see are shown below:

ๆ	When you see this, it means the previous word needs to be repeated.
ฯ	This sign means that the preceding word is an abbreviation.
◌์	This sign makes the letter it is above silent.
ฯลฯ	This sign has the same effect as 'etc' does in the English language.

Appendix F. Full List of Consonants and Their Meaning

Once you've progressed past the consonant sounds, classes, vowel sounds, tone marks, etc., you're probably going to want to learn the actual consonant names. It's not advisable to do this until you're sure you're ready, as the sounds shapes (and classes) are far more important at the early stage; but, it's handy to know the consonant names as you progress.

First, if you ask or someone asks you how to spell a word; and, secondly, if you want to use a Thai dictionary. One thing which very few books will help you with is the consonant order. With the English alphabet we consider it simple, "*A, B, C, D, E, F...*" and so forth, with the Thai alphabet, as you're aware, this is not so.

This is what gave Russ the idea for *Learning Thai, Your Great Adventure* (and that book gave us the idea for this book). Russ simply couldn't remember the consonant order. There were no books that address this, LTYGA does. If you really want to learn to speak, read and write Thai, then we would, of course, thoroughly recommend that book to you.

No.	Thai Consonant	Transliterated Thai Name	Meaning	Initial Consonant Sound	Final Consonant Sound
1	ก ไก่	Gɔɔ Gài	Chicken	/g/	/k/
2	ข ไข่	Kɔ̌ɔ Kài	Egg	/k/	
3	ฃ ขวด	Kɔ̌ɔ Kùat	Bottle	/k/	
4	ค ควาย	Kɔɔ Kwaai	Buffalo	/k/	
5	ฅ คน	Kɔɔ Kon	Person	/k/	
6	ฆ ระฆัง	Kɔɔ Rá-kang	Bell	/k/	
7	ง งู	Ngɔɔ Nguu	Snake	/ng/	
8	จ จาน	Jɔɔ Jaan	Plate	/j/	/t/
9	ฉ ฉิ่ง	Chɔ̌ɔ Chìng	Cymbals	/ch/	/t/
10	ช ช้าง	Chɔɔ Cháang	Elephant	/ch/	/t/
11	ซ โซ่	Sɔɔ Sôo	Chain	/s/	/t/

12	ฌ เฌอ	Chɔɔ Chəə	Tree	/ch/	/t/
13	ญ หญิง	Yɔɔ Yĭng	Woman	/y/	/n/
14	ฎ ชฎา	Dɔɔ Chá-daa	Head-dress	/d/	/t/
15	ฏ ปฏัก	Dtɔɔ Bpà-dtàk	Spear	/dt/	/t/
16	ฐ ฐาน	Tɔɔ Tăan	Pedestal	/t/	
17	ฑ มณโฑ	Tɔɔ Montoo	Giant's Wife	/t/	
18	ฒ ผู้เฒ่า	Tɔɔ Pûu-tâo	Old Man	/t/	
19	ณ เณร	Nɔɔ Neen	Monk	/n/	
20	ด เด็ก	Dɔɔ Dèk	Child	/d/	/t/
21	ต เต่า	Dtɔɔ Dtào	Turtle	/dt/	/t/
22	ถ ถุง	Tɔɔ Tŭng	Bag	/t/	
23	ท ทหาร	Tɔɔ Tá-hăan	Soldier	/t/	
24	ธ ธง	Tɔɔ Tong	Flag	/t/	
25	น หนู	Nɔɔ Nŭu	Mouse	/n/	
26	บ ใบไม้	Bɔɔ Bai-mái	Leaf	/b/	/p/
27	ป ปลา	Bpɔɔ Bplaa	Fish	/bp/	/p/
28	ผ ผึ้ง	Pɔɔ Pʉng	Bee	/p/	
29	ฝ ฝา	Fɔɔ Făa	Lid	/f/	/p/
30	พ พาน	Pɔɔ Paan	Tray	/p/	
31	ฟ ฟัน	Fɔɔ Fan	Tooth	/f/	/p/
32	ภ สำเภา	Pɔɔ Sămpao	Junk	/p/	
33	ม ม้า	Mɔɔ Máa	Horse	/m/	
34	ย ยักษ์	Yɔɔ Yák	Giant	/y/	/i/
35	ร เรือ	Rɔɔ Rʉʉa	Boat	/r/	/n/
36	ล ลิง	Lɔɔ Ling	Monkey	/l/	/n/

37	ว แหวน	Wɔɔ Wɛ̌ɛn	Ring	/w/	/o/
38	ศ ศาลา	Sɔ̌ɔ Sǎa-laa	Tent	/s/	/t/
39	ษ ฤๅษี	Sɔ̌ɔ R~~uu~~-sǐi	Hermit	/s/	/t/
40	ส เสือ	Sɔ̌ɔ S~~ʉ~~ʉa	Tiger	/s/	/t/
41	ห หีบ	Hɔ̌ɔ Hìip	Chest	/h/	
42	ฬ จุฬา	Lɔɔ Jù-laa	Star-shaped Kite	/l/	/n/
43	อ อ่าง	ɔɔ Àang	Bowl	/ɔɔ/	
44	ฮ นกฮูก	Hɔɔ Nók-hûuk	Owl	/h/	

Appendix G. Full List of Vowels

The following tables show the full list of vowels:

Appendix G.1 Simple Vowels

Short Vowel			Long Vowel		
Vowel	Sound	Sounds Like	Vowel	Sound	Sounds Like
The 4 vowels to the right can be short or long but are considered long for tone purposes.			-ํา	/am/	umbrella
			ใ -	/ai/	knight
			ไ -	/ai/	fly
			เ - า	/ao/	mouse
- ะ	/a/	puffin	- า	/aa/	palm
ิ	/i/	lip	ี	/ii/	steeple
ึ	/ʉ/	push-up	ื	/ʉʉ/	bloom
ุ	/u/	crook	ู	/uu/	boot
เ - ะ	/e/	net	เ -	/ee/	bed
แ - ะ	/ɛ/	trap	แ -	/ɛɛ/	mare
โ - ะ	/o/	cot	โ -	/oo/	ghost
เ - าะ	/ɔ/	slot	- อ	/ɔɔ/	awful

Appendix G.2 Complex Vowels

Short Vowel			Long Vowel		
Vowel	Sound	Sounds Like	Vowel	Sound	Sounds Like
เ - อะ	/ə/	above	เ - อ	/əə/	early
เ◌̅ ยะ	/ia/	ria	เ◌̅ ย	/iia/	reindeer
เ◌̅ อะ	/ɯa/	newer	เ◌̅ อ	/ɯɯa/	Skua
◌̆ วะ	/ua/	buat	◌̆ ว	/uua/	pure
ฤ	/rɯ/	rook	ฤๅ	/rɯɯ/	root
ฦ	/lɯ/	lookout	ฦๅ	/lɯɯ/	looney

Your Notes

A Note From the Authors

Just before you reach the lat page, Duangta and I would like to wholeheartedly thank you for placing your trust in us and our *Quest system* by buying this book; alternatively, you could have also obtained it as a freebie when you bought the **Learn Thai Alphabet Application**; but, whatever the case, thank you for reading this far through it and we really hope that it has made learning the Thai alphabet easy for you.

Indeed, some customers have written to us and told us how easy it did was for them and if it has had a similar effect on you, then we'd be dleighted to to hear from you.

We stand by our system and what we say and do, and have put enormous time and effort into creating what we feel is **the** best system for learning Thai. At the time of writing, there isn't any other system like it on the market.

Before we go, we would like to ask a small favour from you, and that is to ask if you would be so kind as to leave a review on Amazon (or wherever you bought the book) as it's reviews from customers which help others take the leap of faith that you yourself did; and, without assistance from people like you, Indie publishers and new writers like us will never get off the ground.

Alternatively, if you would like to pen a few words as a testimonial for us to use on the website, in our other products (we are in the process of creating more), then: 1) it will be of great help to us and our potential customers; and 2) we <u>always</u> remember those who have taken the time to help us and our products.

On the next pages are reminders of the other products in *Quest* and, before we close, we would just like to wish you all the success in your studies and in learning Thai.

Kind regards,

Russ & Duangta

russ@learnthaialphabet.com

Our Quest Products

The products in *Quest* system are:

Volume I - Learning Thai, Your Great Adventure is the
place to start your Quest. Introducing the Thai language,
the alphabet: the consonants, classes and sounds, vowels,
tone, why it's important; and so much more.

***Volume II - Learn Thai Alphabet with Memory Aids to
Your Great Adventure*** is the book that makes learning the
Thai alphabet so simple: it couldn't get any easier.

Volume III - The Perfect Thai Phrasebook is for those
who not only want an accompaniment on their trip to the
Land of Smiles, but is for those who, when they realise (as
you did) that they want to learn more about Thailand, its
language and its culture, can then use it as an aide-memoir
to learning to read Thai: packed with everyday words, phrases, and
expressions, that people actually use.

Volume IV - How to Read Thai is the book that makes
reading Thai not only a reality, but easy. We guide you step-
by-step through the process of breaking down Thai
sentences into words, and words into syllables. It might
sound crazy, but Thai has few spaces and puntuation and
the answer to the common questionof , *"Where or how do you start?"* is no
longer a mystery.

The Learn Thai Alphabet Application

The Learn Thai Alphabet Application

Some screenshots from the application showing the interface, consonants, consonant classes, vowels, rockstars (hard) level, tone marks, test results, audio, etc.

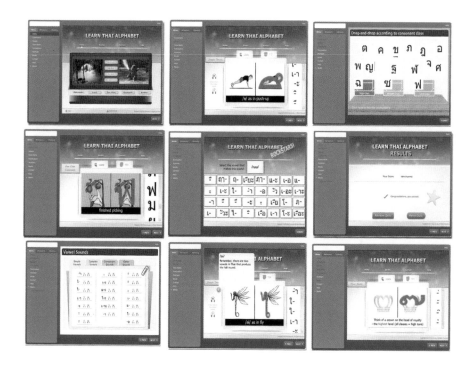

www.learnthaialphabet.com

Made in the USA
Lexington, KY
09 September 2016